MW00574269

THE
PATCHWORKS
OF
LUCY BOSTON

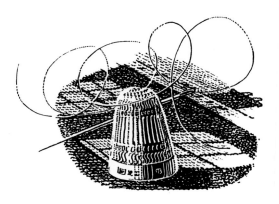

"They ought to be almost like
reading poetry, going from one word
to the next and making a verse."
Lucy Boston, 1980

THE PATCHWORKS OF LUCY BOSTON

Diana Boston

PHOTOGRAPHS BY
Julia Hedgecoe

COLT BOOKS
CAMBRIDGE
in association with Oldknow Books

Colt Books Ltd
9 Clarendon Road
Cambridge CB2 2BH
Tel: (01223) 329059
Fax: (01223) 65866

This edition first published by
Colt Books Ltd 1995
in association with Oldknow Books

British Library Cataloguing in Publications Data
A catalogue record for this book is available from the British Library

ISBN 0 905899 21 0

Drawings by Peter Boston

Designed by Clare Byatt

Colour origination and typesetting in Palatino
by Goodfellow & Egan Ltd., Cambridge

Printed and bound by Proost NV, Belgium

*Frontispiece: The Patchwork of the Crosses on the bed in
the guest room, The Manor, Hemingford Grey*

Contents

Acknowledgements

I SHOULD like to record my special gratitude to my husband Peter for his careful proof-reading and honing of the text and his patient humour over my erratic grammar and spelling; Caroline Hemming for the loan of Lucy's letters and for sharing with me her intimate knowledge of the creation of the patchworks; Julia Hedgecoe for the splendid photographs taken with infinite patience in the face of much malevolence from inanimate objects; Margaret Clark, Caroline Hemming, Ronald Lewcock and Colin Tilney for lending me their patchworks to be photographed; Stella Lucy for giving me the black and white photographs and Jill Paton Walsh for printing them; Nigel Chancellor for the invaluable loan of his barn as a photographic studio; Robert and Linda Yeatman for their unstinting help, advice and encouragement; the Committee of Region Nine of the Quilters' Guild and the Cromwell Quilters for their generous contributions towards the publication costs of this book.

Diana Boston
Hemingford Grey, February 1995

The children's room at The Manor, Hemingford Grey with Kate's Stars patchwork on the bed.

Lucy Boston and her Patchworks

LUCY Boston's first patchworks were made in 1938 when she was living at 15 King's Parade, Cambridge. She made two, a curtain and a cover to be thrown over a sofa. They were simple, bold, straightforward rosettes of large regular hexagons in fairly muted colours. These both went with her to The Manor, Hemingford Grey shortly afterwards.

As restoration of this ancient house progressed, her attention began to focus on the need to furnish it. Lucy, her artist friend Elisabeth Vellacott and her son Peter, when he was at home, all joined in the production of furnishing fabrics using potatoes and lino blocks. Elisabeth Vellacott's potato-print and sequin curtains still hang in front of a cupboard in the hall and Lucy's scallop shell lino-block curtains hang in the guest-room.

As well as curtains, bedcovers were needed. It was by now wartime, and fabrics were difficult to find, but Lucy had always been a tireless and enterprising seamstress and must have saved remnants. Favourites of these were cut into squares and pieced together as bedspreads. She made two such bedspreads at this time, one to cover a single bed and one for a double bed.

For Lucy music was essential, and she had accumulated a vast collection of 78 rpm classical gramophone records, largely purchased during her three years self-imposed exile in Italy and Austria. These had been brought home at

considerable risk of rupture to countless continental railway and cross-channel ferry porters. Towards the end of 1941 she wrote to the Welfare Officer at nearby RAF Wyton suggesting that the men might perhaps like to come over to the Manor once a week to listen to music if they were not night-flying. The station padre visited Lucy and was enthusiastic, and said he would arrange for a bus-load to come.

With only one sofa and a few Regency dining-room chairs, Lucy had nowhere for a bus-load of men to sit in comfort, but, as with her early patchworks, she pieced together what she had. Mattresses were covered with bedspreads; pillows were covered with various fabrics to turn them into cushions, and placed with other large cushions that she had already upholstered with hairy brown-and-white calf skins from her husband's tannery. She solved the problem of furnishing an alcove under one of the Norman windows by wrapping a mattress round the wall and filling in the floor space inside it with the back seat of her car. Fifty-three years on this is still in the same place. By the time she had finished, the room had a very medieval look, furnished as if for returning crusaders. Her brother, Jas, with characteristic fraternal irreverence, described it as "Lucy's fur-lined Valhalla".

These record recitals continued throughout the war years and were so popular that they became twice-weekly events. At this stage of her life, she was too busy to paint or sew. Her patchworking did not start again until after the war, when she made a beautiful cot cover in silk.

The curtain in the dining-room at The Manor, Hemingford Grey

The creation of her main patchworks did not begin in earnest until the mid 1950s and the ideas for these must have grown gradually.

Black-and-white photographs of the house in the early 1940s show that Lucy had already bought a very large old patchwork for use as a bedcover in the guest-room. A little later she bought another which is composed of small hexagon rosettes and is very weighty with its interlining of sheep's wool and a thick backing. It is very heavily quilted,

The lining to the High Magic Patchwork

presumably to keep the sheep's wool evenly spread. Two of the small hexagons bear the inscriptions, in a neat italic hand in rather faded black ink, "begun 1801" and "completed 1803". This quilt was found to fit perfectly as a curtain for one of the west windows in the dining-room, while the other quilt (off the guest-room bed) turned out to be exactly the right size for a floor-to-ceiling curtain over the south French windows in the same room. Elisabeth Vellacott tracked down a single-bed patchwork which Lucy bought and hung as a curtain over the third dining-room window. With the fire lit, and these beautiful, old, heavy quilts drawn, blotting out draughts and external noise, there is still a feeling of peace and total security in this tranquil thick-walled room, in which the relentless noises of the twentieth century intrude only as a barely perceptible murmur high up in the massive chimney.

With constant use, being pulled to and fro each day, and under the destructive influence of light and wood-smoke, these patchworks inevitably suffered from wear and tear. Winter after winter, Lucy restored them with new appropriate fabric until the curtain patchworks became almost entirely made by her. She was still repairing them when she was in her nineties, for she wrote to her niece, Caroline Hemming, "I am mending the old ones and find I can sew, but it's rather hit or miss. Damn my eyes. I could keep my spirits up if I could see." Sitting in the dining-room, facing the big curtain when it is drawn at night, I have been able to see where many of her early ideas for patchwork originated.

The centre of this large curtain is a six-foot square filled with clusters of rosettes. It seems that Lucy's first repairs followed the maker's patterns. She used fabric of a similar colour fairly randomly cut. Then her ideas changed, and she began to cut out hexagons with more thought for the final result so that the pattern in the fabric created new patterns in the patchwork. Stripes were matched to create new hexagons within the rosettes or were lined up to radiate from the centre of the rosettes. Floral patterns were cut out with the same flower in the centre of each hexagon. This marshalling of the pattern in the fabric to create a new doubly-intricate pattern in the patchwork became Lucy's hallmark.

Averil Colby was a master of this technique, and Lucy certainly had her book *Patchwork*, but only the fifth impression, published in 1967. Many of the repairs in the big dining-room curtain, her first small template patchwork and the rosettes applied to the Huckabuck Patchwork, predate this edition, so it is probable that Lucy herself thought up this intensification of patterns. Some of her later masterpieces were undoubtedly influenced by Averil Colby's book.

In Jill Paton Walsh's introduction to Lucy's two autobiographies, *Memories*, she writes how Lucy, in her sixties, along with William Mayne and Philippa Pearce, C S Lewis and Rosemary Sutcliffe, "was fully in touch with the spirit of the times, and was one of a galaxy of talented writers, exploring and mapping the possibilities of children's books as fully serious literature." It seems that this is also true of her patchworks where, probably without knowing it, she was following the trend that was being encouraged by Averil Colby.

From the repair of the dining-room curtains Lucy learnt how easily fabrics wore out, so she took care never to use *worn* clothes or furnishing fabrics in her own patchworks. They are all made with unused remnants left over from garments, chaircovers or curtains made by her, or from new

1,000 1" hexagons, 1,000 1" long diamond cards, a set of templates to make a 16-pointed star, a set of templates to make a fine-pointed star and 100 2" diamond cards.

Lucy was not someone who kept copies of her orders so this was most probably never sent, as it is still tucked into the A.J. Scott catalogue, a booklet entitled *Patchwork* (undated). The order must have been written when she was contemplating making the High Magic Patchwork.

The Scott catalogue contains basic instructions for making patchwork. As well as being a guide to choosing templates, it has a wide range of template patterns together with the designs that can be built from them. Although Lucy ordered a thousand cards at a time, with her careful stitching and careful removal these cards could be re-used. Amongst her patchwork equipment there are many of these re-used cards with tiny perforations round the edge and tacking holes. One of the A.J. Scott lists gives the price of the long hexagon and the octagon cards at 10d for fifty and the squares at 6d for fifty. Later, it became far too expensive to buy the machine-cut cards (quoted as being 55p for fifty in a later catalogue) so she would make her own, sometimes allowing friends who could cut accurately to help her. These were cut out of Company Annual Reports, until it became the fashion to make these coloured and glossy and impossible to use! Lucy then resorted to *Basildon Bond* writing paper; she was particularly attracted to the lined page from the front of each pad, finding that the guide-lines helped the scissors to produce accurate geometric shapes.

With most of the patchworks she would concentrate on a single block and then put it aside in one of the large, flat, round baskets that were always beside her when she worked. Each block was a miniature work of art achieved by imaginative cutting and placing of the fabric. Her success in achieving this careful matching is all the more extraordinary when one remembers that all the patches were joined back to back.

All her early patchworks are sewn using twenty stitches to the inch. They look as if they were sewn by The Tailor of Gloucester. Looking at them, it is hard to believe that they were made in the very dark dining-room of her ancient house, and in winter when it is even darker. All were sewn by artificial light. The hands that created these incredibly fine patchworks were not the dainty little hands that you might imagine sewing twenty stitches to the inch; they were large, practical, square-fingered hands, the colour of old teak, hard and rough from vigorous weeding and the firm planting of trees and roses in the garden. Peter Gunn describes them in *Lucy Boston Remembered*:

> What was immediately remarkable were her hands, large, gnarled and weathered, masculine, like those of a competent artisan.

She would often not decide what fabric, or arrangement of template shapes, to use to join the blocks together until she had finished enough blocks for the bed cover. She would then lay them out, decide what colour she needed and either shop for it herself or put out an SOS to her friends until exactly the right fabric was found.

Lucy sewed her patchworks sitting in her armchair by the dining-room fire, so all the blocks were made on her knee. When they were completed, she would lay them out

Diana Boston in the main bedroom at The Manor, Hemingford Grey

either on the floor or on the double bed in the spare room, and move them around until she felt that they were correctly placed in relation to each other. She would then start on the rather less imaginative but equally exciting work of joining them all together into the final composition. In 1980, when she was eighty-eight years old and finishing the Needlecord Patchwork, she wrote in a letter to Caroline Hemming:

> I have practically finished mine but rank it low. It is obvious, not intriguing. They ought to be almost like reading poetry, going from one word to the next and making a verse.

As the patchwork grew, this operation would move from her lap to the dining-room table. Most of the patchworks were then mounted on to a border and lined with carefully chosen fabric. This process was also enjoyed, as she wrote to Caroline:

> Thank you for launching me on the new patchwork. I have sewn most of your squares together and am itching to start a flower, but enjoy hemming the lining on the other.

Until, finally, as in another letter to Caroline:

> The patchwork is finished and edged but not yet lined. I am waiting for the lining and meanwhile can't imagine how I lived when I wasn't patching. It is flatter than finishing a book.

While her fingers were busy stitching, she must often have been planning her books. Another letter:

> I am writing like one fiend-driven, partly because of

Introduction
written by Lucy Boston

for an exhibition of her patchworks
organised by Christopher Hogwood
at Kings Lynn in 1976

*P*ATCHWORK is a very old craft, but came into its greatest popularity when cotton was introduced to Europe from India. There had been quilts in linen, sometimes in two colours only, and in silk. One of the most beautiful I ever saw was in white bridal silk only, gaining great richness of texture by the sewing together of tiny equal diamonds. In the days when nearly all clothes were made at home, there would always be mountains of bits, and a family of girls could all work on it together. The bridal quilt would be part of one's trousseau, one's former life all incorporated in it. It has been said that the paper templates should properly be from one's love letters, but if so it would have to be a long engagement and an unsentimental one. Fancy cutting them up!

There are a great many simple traditional patterns with names like "Star of Bethlehem", "Everlasting Tree", "Waves", etc., and from America, "Log Cabin". These are good designs and capable of almost endless variation, but of course it is more fun to do one's own.

Linen is heavy and more difficult to sew. Silk perishes too

Lucy's sewing paraphernalia

easily at the seams. Cotton must be fine and firm. A lot of Indian cottons, though splendid in design, are much too loosely woven and the bias pulls out of shape. Liberty lawn is surprisingly and excellently firm and durable but should not be mixed with heavy cottons.

It is a fallacy that in patchwork any colour goes. The pleasure of the work comes from using one's own choice of colour for each two little pieces one sews together, as a painter would. A desperate search through tumbled masses of bits for the right tone is often necessary, and one can only use what one has. Consequently the occupation is disorderly and messy, the room littered with snippets of paper, cotton and lengths of thread, and a maelstrom of materials. You need lots of large baskets and polythene bags in which to put your templates and the patches already mounted on paper. Traditionally, one needle should do the whole quilt, and it shapes itself into a curve most convenient for oversewing. This should be twenty stitches to the inch, which becomes quite habitual.

The work should always be bordered with a straight edge so that the weight of the whole never comes on a sewn joint. Test your material for fraying on a cut edge. Real cotton does not fray even on the bias; modern imitations fray so badly as to be not worth sewing.

The Patchworks

The Large Hexagon Patchwork

*T*HIS is an attractive, simple patchwork which came with Lucy to the Manor from her lodgings at 15 King's Parade in Cambridge, and since then has always been used over the sofa in the music-room where it is perfectly attuned to the muted pinks and greys of the ancient plaster and stonework. For this patchwork Lucy used linens, choosing different colours to form simple rosettes. The patchwork is finished off at the edge with templates cut from a finer linen than that used for the centre. None of Lucy's patchworks is interlined but this one is quilted through to the backing with the quilting following the outline of the rosettes.

It is a subtle combination of delicate colours: cinnamon pink, cream, stone grey, Indian red, and watercress, which fuse cool salad-like freshness into a composition which appears modestly unassuming yet is sumptuous enough to be spread for Cleopatra's reclining.

The Large Hexagon Patchwork
Length: 93"   *Width:* 70"   *Templates:* 2½" hexagons
Lining: Cream cotton folded over to the front to form a border on to which the patchwork is mounted, leaving a ¼" band round the edge
Date: 1938

The Huckabuck Patchwork

*T*HIS double bed quilt was originally made with squares of a flower-print cotton, of the type used for the wrap-around pinafores of the time, alternately spaced with white squares cut from huckabuck face-towels and table-napkins; it was then bordered, lined and quilted through to the back diagonally in both directions across each square.

This is how it must have remained for a time. However, to repair the big dining-room curtain Lucy had to make new rosettes based on one central 1" hexagon surrounded by six of the same. She was inspired to make more rosettes than were necessary for the curtains, and these she later mounted on to the white huckabuck and table-napkin

Length: 84" *Width:* 107" *Templates:* 6½" squares and 1" hexagons
Border: an 8" band of the checked seersucker turned back on itself to form an 8½" border round the lining
Lining: Fairly loosely woven cotton; possibly a wartime sheet as there are no seams
Date: The basic patchwork of squares was probably made in the early 1940s

squares of this wartime patchwork. She added a further four hexagons to the rosettes to fill the corner of each of the white squares.

This demonstrates Lucy's early experiments in creating new patterns from the fabric prints or weave achieved by both deliberate cutting and placing of the hexagons, often using the same fabric to create quite different patterns. An example in this patchwork can be seen in her several uses of the white fabric with pink scallop-shapes and grey flowers. There are six different ways in which this fabric is used on its own and a further two where it is used with a toning print. She also used the green and yellow versions of this same material.

When she had finished applying the rosettes Lucy again quilted through to the backing, this time following the rosette shapes. This and the King's Parade patchworks are the only ones she quilted all over.

Clearly to be seen in this photograph is the use of three different colours of the same print. All Lucy's patchworks are sewn by hand, even the piecing together of these large squares.

Some of these silks, used in the Silk Cot Cover, must date from before the second world war and a few remnants of them were still amongst Lucy's patchwork material when she died in 1990, including a silk handkerchief made from the very same material from which the black and cream diamonds at the top of this photograph were cut.

Ivy Leaf
Patchwork

I HAVE never seen this patchwork and only discovered its existence early in 1994 when a neighbour, Stella Lucy, telephoned to introduce herself and to invite me to coffee to see some photographs she had of Lucy Boston. I was excited to see that the photographs showed this patchwork, used as a bedcover. Its present whereabouts are unknown; however, its last known owner lived in Bath so it may still exist in that area.

I have looked at the photographs with the aid of a magnifying glass and recognise many of the fabrics from the other patchworks. Her son, Peter, who had forgotten it until seeing the photographs, believes it was finished in 1956.

It seems that, as in the Huckabuck Patchwork, the blocks are applied to squares of white fabric alternating with squares of a grey-green ivy leaf print left over from curtains made in 1952 for Peter's home in Highgate.

The bedcover is divided into three sections separated by 'barley sugar' stripes made up of alternating long hexagon patches of striped fabric and patches of a dark leaf print. These dark stripes are bordered on either side with pieced spotted fabric; I suspect that this is a pale duck egg blue with a pin-head sized red dot, since a similar fabric was used in several of the patchworks and Lucy also used it to make two simple summer quilts.

A rare photograph of Lucy with one of her patchworks.

Each section consists of three rows of twelve squares in which the patchwork appliqué squares and the ivy leaf print squares alternate. The border is made up of two of the 'barley sugar' stripes edged with the presumed duck egg blue fabric separated by a row of white hexagons.

The actual patchwork blocks appear to be made using a variety of approximately 1" template shapes. All the star patterns are formed with a central hexagon surrounded by an irregular pentagon, three sides of which are the same as the hexagon, the other two being longer and forming a triangle. (This shape is sometimes referred to as a 'bishop's mitre'.) These star patterns are then finished off with six hexagons between the points of the stars. Other blocks are hexagon rosettes with an outer ring of six hexagons; a few are a mixture of hexagons and diamonds so joined that they form a large octagon.

Lucy's first four patchworks had been made with either simple squares or large 2½″ hexagons. The repairs to the dining-room curtain had then started Lucy's interest in using smaller shapes. This was when she applied the decoration to the Huckabuck Patchwork and made the Silk Cot Cover, which is entirely of diamonds. When embarking on this lost bedcover she obviously tried out new template shapes and new combinations of shapes. The various experiments pieced together here are the seeds of later, grander ideas.

The variety of combinations and templates, the barley-sugar stripes and the ivy leaf pattern, can all be seen in this photograph of The Ivy Leaf Patchwork hanging over a screen, given to me by Stella Lucy.

The Patchwork of the Crosses

*T*HIS is the first of Lucy's major post-war patchworks, made when she was in her sixties. The blocks are constructed from long hexagons often called 'church windows'. The original plan for this was sketched out by Lucy very roughly in the A. J. Scott catalogue [see Lucy Boston and her Patchworks, pp. 10–11]. Each of the fifty-six blocks is carefully executed using twenty-four 'church windows' worked into the various patterns, mostly based on different crosses. These blocks are surrounded by a single border of long hexagons in creamy-white cotton. Cut with the warp running the length of the shape and then placed around the block they catch the light differently and shimmer like pearl.

Length: 88″   *Width:* 99″   *Templates:* 1″ long hexagons and 1″ squares
Border: Marbled-brown print with a red stripe, folded on the red stripe and carefully mitred at the corner to form a narrow red border. This is then folded back on itself to form a 5¼″ border round the lining
Lining: A delicately printed floral lawn in two pieces joined across the width
Date: Unknown, but probably the late 1950s

now rather frail, wall-hanging. It has a definite ecclesiastical flavour, due as much to the colouring and the patterns as to any religious or architectural overtones arising out of the colloquial term for long hexagons. Lucy achieved a perfect balance in the placing of the blocks, and what is more, managed this without ever being able to get far enough away from it to see what the overall effect would be from a distance. I have had the privilege of being able to see the effect of her work when the patchwork was mounted on a large vertical screen to be photographed for this book.

Lucy wrote of this patchwork for the King's Lynn exhibition:

> Interesting patterns can be made by cutting out particular details in the material and using them to make symmetrical figures of their own. This, of course, means very wasteful cutting whereas the original notion of patchwork was economy. Note that there are only two basic shapes in this.

The stitching is so fine, and the positioning of the stripes on the twelve elongated hexagons cut from the delightful black, white and green striped floral print is so precise that it is almost impossible to make out the template shapes in this block. The four pairs of patches on the outer diagonals of the cross are cut from fabric used much later as the breast of the thrush on p.69.

Toby Hemming's Cot Cover

C AROLINE Hemming had always dreamed of Lucy sitting in the inglenook at the Manor sewing a patchwork of the colours of the fire. Her dream was realised when Lucy dashed this off in time for the birth of Caroline's first baby, Toby. The grey and white seersucker represents the smoke with the eighty-five stars as the various colours of flames and sparks.

The whole patchwork is made using one template and all the fabrics have been used before in the Patchwork of the Crosses and the Huckabuck Patchwork. The stars are six-pointed, connected with the 'smoke' diamonds. Although well-used and washed, so that some of the fiery colours have faded considerably, this patchwork is still very beautiful.

Appliquéd on to the back of the lining are four stars of different blues with a touch of grey; a charming detail.

Length: 46″   Width: 38″   Template: 1½″ diamond
Border: ½″ bright blue fabric folded on centre of black squares to make a pattern of triangles. This same fabric forms a 2″ border to the lining.
Lining: Narrow-lined grey and white check seersucker
Date: Summer 1957

The back of Toby Hemming's Cot Cover. This combination of blues with the pale grey lining is fresh and pleasing. The care that went into the composition of each pattern was exercised equally in the choice of backing material with the result that the reverse of every patchwork would in itself make a very desirable bedcover.

High Magic Patchwork

SIR Martin Ryle, the Astronomer Royal, was a very close friend of Lucy's. Lady Ryle described him as a star in Lucy's firmament. Lucy was always fascinated by natural *coups-de-théâtre* such as eruptions, earthquakes and thunderstorms, so it was inevitable that she should relish long conversations with him about the more cataclysmic aspects of astronomy and such awesome concepts as the 'Big Bang'. This High Magic Patchwork was inspired both by these conversations and by the various star patterns in the A. J. Scott catalogue.

During one of the winters while she was making this patchwork she was also writing *An Enemy at Green Knowe*, a book full of magic and dedicated to Claire, Martin Ryle's daughter. While her hands were busy creating her patchworks, her thoughts were often engaged in planning her books. In both, her attention to detail, the extra touches to perfect the work, is that of a painter at work in another medium – words or fabrics.

This patchwork consists of nine 14" central blocks, each one surrounded and linked by a border of six-pointed stars in a background of hexagons cut from a blue, purple-and-brown mottled fabric; a perfect choice for a midnight sky. Lucy found another blue material printed with white stars of the exact size to fit the centre of the hexagon template

the pattern run across the triangle, giving the impression of rings round the suns. The colours are hot and exciting, quite different from the large frosty stars in the opposite two corner blocks.

The central block is the 'Star of Bethlehem' based on a 1¼" long diamond, and created with a careful choice and the usual precise inclusion of pattern variations. She used the background midnight fabrics for the outer edges of the star, and then applied the whole to a 14" square of the midnight fabric. The central block of the patchwork is sewn through to the lining around the outer edge of the star. When hand-sewing together the border of the backing Lucy caught down the patchwork in strategic places where hexagons joined. This stitching is completely invisible on the front. All the seams of the lining are sewn by hand.

The two remaining stars were made using the templates from the sixteen-pointed star set, except that the infills are made from the long diamonds rather than the very much simpler templates supplied by A.J. Scott. These stars are also applied to 14" squares of the midnight fabric, so that they appear to hang in an infinite void.

The four blue blocks were made by piecing ¾" octagons and squares, using four different blue fabrics for the octagons. On three of these blocks Lucy was dissatisfied with the starry effect and embroidered simple stars on to the squares. The squares of the fourth block were cut from fabric printed with small stars in a variety of sizes.

The stars bordering the nine main blocks are white, red, yellow, pink, blue and grey. Every diamond is cut with great care so that stripes join at the centre, radiating out to the points. Other patterns match across the joins. Many of the fabrics may be seen in the other patchworks but a couple are unique to this one, appearing as single stars. They

*A mixture of printed stars, embroidered stars, appliquéd stars and
pieced stars combine to show Lucy's artistic skill in creating a truly
dramatic patchwork. The 'midnight sky' base fabric creeps in between
two points of the large, frosty star where, presumably, the deep blue
fabric had run out.*

THE PATCHWORKS OF LUCY BOSTON

may have been samples or remnants given to Lucy. There is no obvious pattern or symmetry in the placing of the stars.

The phases of the moon are all pieced, except some of the thinnest crescent moons. The full moons are made with a central circle surrounded by sixteen truncated triangles. These sets of moons are made out of four separate fabrics, so that they all have different degrees of clarity, as though seen through fog, interstellar matter, dust, or on a clear frosty night.

This is the most imaginative of Lucy's patchworks; a wonderful mixture of template shapes and techniques. Putting it all together must have been like making a giant jigsaw puzzle – often having to create novel shapes to accommodate awkward corners. The insertion of the nine blocks into the hexagons required some unusual adaptations of the hexagon template, particularly round the edge of the blue blocks. The adaptation of these shapes, and the creation of the moons with the truncated triangles, presented no problem to Lucy, who always maintained that the creation of patchworks was the only possible use that she could have for mathematics.

In a letter to Caroline Hemming she wrote:

The patchwork is pure happiness.

This letter is undated, so that we cannot know to which patchwork she is referring, but she must certainly have exulted in the composition of this one.

Lucy wrote of this patchwork for the King's Lynn exhibition:

This was done while I was writing a book for children about magic. It served to keep my thoughts moving.

This block is made up of ¾″ octagons (from the bright blue and black fabric bordering the previous cot cover) and ¾″ squares. Four-pointed white stars are pieced in amongst these, necessitating some inventive re-shaping of the adjacent octagons.

The Keyboard Patchwork

*T*HE inspiration for this bedcover was possibly a photograph in Averil Colby's book of 'A Devonshire quilt with a centre pattern of square and octagonal pieces *c*. 1870.' Lucy owned the fifth impression of this book, printed in 1967, and it is likely that the patchwork was started that winter.

The combination of octagons and squares used in this patchwork is not very popular with quilters because of the work involved in piecing it together. This patchwork is therefore truly remarkable as the sides of the octagons and squares are only ¾". It must have required medieval patience to cut out the fabric, let alone to sew all the pieces together. There are one hundred and fifty-four blocks, which means 1,386 of those little squares tacked on to

Length: 92"   *Width:* 76"   *Templates:* ¾" octagons and ¾" squares
Border: A dark print fabric with stripes of circles and zigzags in black, blue and brown. It is folded back on itself to form a 7½" border framing the patchwork and a 9" border round the lining
Lining: A very dainty, attractive blue floral and butterfly print on white, in two pieces joined down the centre
Date: Probably started in 1967, when Lucy was 75

when discussing her work with Caroline Hemming, Lucy said, 'A woman's job is to create circles of affection.'

Lucy wrote of this patchwork for the King's Lynn exhibition:

A direct reaction to the flamboyance of its predecessor. An investigation of the colour possibilities of black, white and grey with minute additions of brown and blue. Note the use of one material to make five or six different patterns.

Linear blocks are interspersed with blocks full of movement with an occasional asymmetric pattern which helps to avoid the static sterility which could have resulted from a too rigorous pursuit of uniformity.

Kate's Stars

THIS brightly-coloured patchwork of one hundred and forty-nine stars was made to go on the bed of Lucy's first granddaughter, Kate. It is a repeat of the idea for Toby Hemming's Cot Cover, but with a cream background to the stars. The stars in the middle and the two outer rows are symmetrically placed, as are the nine bright blue stars. The rest are randomly placed with the strong colours carefully balanced.

The pale blue stars show a foretaste of the same overlapping of patterns which she was to exploit so comprehensively in the Kaleidoscope patchwork some three years later.

Lucy wrote of this patchwork for the King's Lynn exhibition:

Simple stars for a granddaughter's bed.

*Length: 79"   **Width:** 53"   **Template:** 1½" diamond*
Border and lining: *Black-and-white floral print consisting of two pieces joined down the centre of the lining, folded over to form the 5½" border down the sides and the 8½" border at either end*
Date: *Probably 1970*

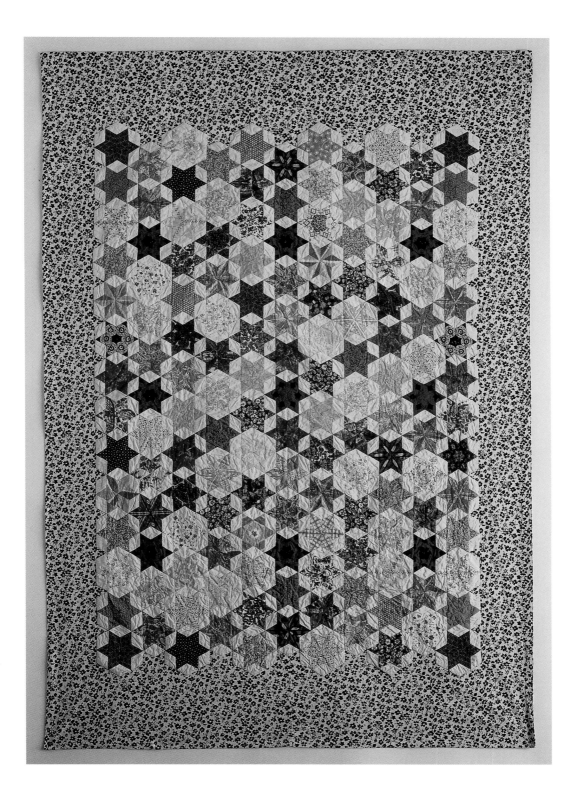

Doll's Cot Stars

*T*HIS charming little patchwork was made for Kate's sixth birthday so that both she and her doll could have matching bedcovers.

The patchwork consists of ten of the six-pointed stars and four three-quarter stars. These are linked with diamonds cut from a fabric printed with white stars and cut so that each diamond has a star in the centre. The whole is then mounted on to a piece of this same fabric. The red diamonds are individually applied to the backing fabric, not pieced into the patchwork. They are cut from the red stripe of the border fabric which, by the time Lucy made this patchwork, had been in her collection for nearly twenty years.

Length: *15½"*　**Width:** *12"*　**Template:** *⅞" diamond*
Border: *The same fabric as The Patchwork of the Crosses folded over to form a marbled border round the lining*
Lining: *White-on-black floral print*
Date: *1974*

from a picture of an American quilt featured in a diary sent to her by her American publisher and great friend Margaret McElderry.

These flowers and the maple leaf shapes are traditionally pieced from diamond templates but Lucy chose to cut them out as one. The layers of the sunflowers at each corner of the patchwork are also cut out in one piece and the edges then turned in. She has adapted the size of the medallion in the middle of each flower to suit the scale of the pattern in the fabric. It is remarkable that eighty-year old fingers could turn in all the edges and sew them down with such invisible stitches and that there is not a thread to be seen in the angles of the maple leaves. The birds' feet, the flower and leaf stalks, all have their edges turned in. The choice of fabrics is wonderfully apt; the feathers on the owl are almost tangible.

The chequer-board is surrounded by a border of stripes similar to pillow-ticking and the ends of the bedspread are extended with squares of Paisley pattern cut from fabric left over from the Patchwork of Crosses. She used the Paisley shape from this material as leaves at the base of the flowers. The patchwork border finishes with a row of dark triangles. There cannot have been enough material to cut triangles for the whole border, so one end is finished with triangles cut from fabric used on the four corners of the moon border of the High Magic Patchwork.

Just as Lucy created the pictures for Harriet's patchwork, 'Friendship Quilts' are often made for a bride by friends each making their own picture on a square which is then sewn into a complete bedcover as a wedding present. In December 1976 Lucy sent just such a square to Caroline Hemming (one of several marvellous little ones). With it went a letter:

Among Lucy's patchwork bits and pieces, I still have her original paper pattern for the owl.

Possibly a friendship quilt can include old crone's sewing. When you consider that I can't see:

the eye of the needle;
the thread (if silko);
the edge of the material;
the point of the needle;
the stitch I have made;

and that in my agony of blindness I even sewed my dressing-gown skirt into it! I did not realise before how much I do the patchwork by touch of the paper edge. It was a revelation of incapacity.

Lucy wrote of this patchwork for the King's Lynn exhibition:

For a younger grandchild with squirrels and birds from my garden.

Many of the fabrics in this patchwork have been used before, so Lucy knew them well and here exploits the illusion of texture in each print. The wings of the thrush are from the same material as the squirrels and its speckled breast, along with the green maple leaves and pale green batik background squares, are all from 1950s fabrics. The red maple leaves are mostly cut from remnants from the High Magic Patchwork fabrics. This is the only patchwork where Lucy uses the brown and green oak leaf batik.

Passacaglia Patchwork

MUSIC and musicians were of enormous importance to Lucy throughout her life, although she was no performer. Colin Tilney, the harpsichordist, became a very close and much-admired friend of hers. Of their first meeting she wrote: 'I have rarely met what I now use the word genius to stand for ... genius is concentric, unforced and of sublime clarity.' Words that describe with extraordinary accuracy this very patchwork made for Colin.

When he emigrated to Canada he housed his Robert Wolfington harpsichord at the Manor, and on his return visits he would play to her and to those lucky enough to

Length: 80"   *Width:* 60"   *Templates:* 1½" squares and 1½" diamonds
Border: Mounted on a 3½" border of the same fabric used to frame the Patchwork of the Crosses, folded over on the red stripe to make a border for the lining
Lining: An unusual damson coloured print with pink cherries
Date: Early 1973

The central block from the reverse of the Passacaglia Patchwork. This charming fruit print used in the four central squares of this block only occurs in one other patchwork. In the repaired dining room curtain there is a single rosette where the six outer hexagons are randomly cut from this fabric, suggesting that it dates from the time when Lucy first started to mend these curtains, before she began to exploit the fabric pattern in her designs.

And a little later:

> The patchwork is finished, except for the edging and lining, it is very beautiful and musical, including your two patterns, and there will be quite a lot of your stuff left. It was marvellously generous of you to hand it over. I will send all your bits back.

Finally:

> The patchwork is lined, signed and untacked. Nothing could have been better than the damson colour.

For the King's Lynn exhibition Lucy wrote:

> Thirty [in fact there are thirty-five] variations on a theme. Made for Colin Tilney as a small thank-offering for playing Frescobaldi's *Hundred Variations in my house.*

Kaleidoscope

*T*HIS patchwork nearly drove Lucy mad with its complexity. On the other hand she found it the most exciting to make, and when complete it replaced the Keyboard Patchwork on her bed. In a letter to Caroline she wrote:

> I am *deep* in Kaleidoscope and can think of nothing else. It requires the brains of a crystallographer and a contrapuntalist, even if the colours required could be bought (I have bought about 20 yards that have proved useless.) However I am up early (5 a.m.) and sit up late in feverish excitement.

This 5 a.m. start was in the winter in an unheated house, where the fire had to be shaken into life before the day's work could begin.

The circular effect in the kaleidoscope starts with an octagon of two fabrics, alternating dark and light, giving an impression of the rotating sails of a windmill. Dark triangles are sewn on the pale sides of each alternate octagon forming the four points of a star, each tip of which touches a neighbouring star. Surrounding the stars are triangles and squares of paler fabrics carefully chosen to give the illusion of circles embracing every star. The circles overlap along the diagonals of the patchwork; interwoven into the overlapping circles appear four-bladed propellers.

As the eye moves across the pattern the emphasis seems to change from interlocking circles running diagonally to propellers running horizontally and vertically. A truly fluid kaleidoscope is thus achieved. The different patterns so blend and intertwine that to see them you must half-close your eyes, letting your eyelashes filter out the different shapes. In this patchwork less use is made of intricate fabric patterns than in other examples of her work. Here movement of pattern is achieved by her choice of shades of colour; producing an overall pearl-like lustre.

Early in 1974, Lucy wrote to Caroline:

HELIOTROPE! Can it really be bought in Falmouth! If so, please send me a pattern. It is the rarest colour and I have just used up a lifetime's reserve of it in finishing this winter's patchwork – very pretty and glittery, but not a classic.

This disillusion with Kaleidoscope did not last so can only have been brought on by winter blues. She writes later in the same letter:

'We live in fogs and rain and I do now feel 81. I never expected to.'

In spite of the difficulty in finding the colours she wanted

Length: 98"   *Width:* 69"   *Templates:* Isosceles triangles, base 1½", sides 2", squares 1½"
Border: A striped black-and-white floral print carefully mitred on the corners, forming an 11½" border folded back on itself to make a 12" border round the lining
Lining: Inside the lining border is a 2¾" band of tartan framing a predominantly lilac print cotton sold for making sheets in the 1970s
Date: 1973 and early 1974

across the middle of them. The Laura Ashley print on which the butterfly is mounted is a perfect match to the border along either side of the picture. It is a splendid boy's bedcover; bold, confident and energetic.

In a letter to Caroline Hemming she wrote:

> I have practically finished, except for the lining, this winter's patchwork, wonderfully barbaric, after Andrew's design.

And later:

> Andrew's patchwork is finished except for the lining. It is wonderful, twelfth-century and unexpected. It took all my primary colours so I am now collecting again, but my eyesight is failing.

Lucy wrote of this patchwork for the King's Lynn exhibition:

> Made for my grandson at his request, the design being the translation into patchwork of a calendar he gave me for Christmas.

Detail of Lucy's patchwork, shown with the calendar that was its inspiration.

Margaret Clark's Ohio Stars

*L*UCY had visited Margaret Clark, her publisher, in her new flat in north London and had been so horrified by this modern building that she decided to make her a patchwork, created to cheer the flat with a design appropriate to a modern setting. Lucy seems to have made this at speed so that Margaret could have it at once.

The actual patchwork measures 69" × 51" and consists of blocks of the pattern known as 'Ohio Star' alternating with blocks of a single fabric. The points of all the stars are cut either from dark brown or dark grey prints giving initially the impression that they are cut from the same material. The background of each star block is cut from very delicate prints on a white ground. The star centres are taken mostly from blue floral prints, but three are from the bright green

Length: 99"   Width: 82"   Templates: Isosceles triangles 1½" base, 1" sides, 1½" squares and 4½" squares
Border: 15" brown-and-white floral print folded back on itself to form 19" border to lining
Lining: Rose-pink floral print
Date: Probably early 1975

bright purple across the corners. These blocks are identical throughout the patchwork.

In each main block the outer ring of long hexagons is in various shades of pale green, and all the squares surrounding both the main blocks and the intersection blocks are cut from the same pink, khaki, and purple Paisley except where Lucy ran out of this material and substituted a fabric of similar colouring. The effect is very regular, and has a rich Victorian opulence.

The pattern blocks are linked throughout with two rows of long hexagons cut from a brown print and divided by a row of Paisley squares on point.

To link the two pattern blocks Lucy had to invent a template that was half a long hexagon, elongated to form the shape children often draw for a house. These are used to finish off the rows between the main block and the block of squares.

In October 1976, she wrote to Caroline:

The patchwork would keep me busy and happy every hour and I wish there was nothing else I ought to do! It goes at a good pace because of all your little trios of green. I would like a yard of each of the enclosed, and send £2. I wonder why Cornwall does so well in patterns. I fear I may run out of the tender donkey-brown.

When nearing completion of this patchwork Lucy wrote again to Caroline:

I am slowly travelling round the border of Colin's immense wallhanging, all in tiny squares. I like it and daily put off my autobiography to sew the little units together.

In one corner of the backing border is stitched a cross of

Lucy was 85 years old when this patchwork was finished but her stitches are still invisible. When sewing the patches together back to back she would do several whipping stitches before pulling the thread through. This not only meant that she sewed with enviable speed but also probably suggests that when her eyesight was not so sharp it was easier to sew by feel.

four long hexagons with 'Colin Tilney', 'with love from', 'Lucy M. Boston', '1976–1977' written on each in linen marker pen.

In February 1977, Lucy wrote:

> He liked his new patchwork: now full double-bed sized.
> Except for parties I want to do nothing else.

Lucy can never have seen this patchwork hung vertically (as for photography) at a distance. Under these conditions it is positively Chartres-like, the patterns glowing like exquisite stained glass in the embrace of brown stone tracery.

Mariner's Compass Patchwork

THIS patchwork was made for my second son, Charles, who was interested in orienteering. This, and the fact that his father lost his life in the Royal Navy, gave Lucy the idea of using the Mariner's Compass pattern. In January 1978 she wrote to Caroline Hemming:

> I miss having a patchwork on hand. Am waiting for templates of Mariner's Compass for Charles, if I can still sew.

As this followed Colin Tilney's wallhanging it is probable that it was of this patchwork that she wrote:

> I thought I would never do another patchwork, blind, but have discovered an irresistible pattern but I too often fail to take in the two edges. I hope Colin's won't fall to bits.

Another letter, dated 26 January 1978, reads:

> I think I told you I was on a new exciting patchwork (pattern called Mariner's Compass) and had done a week's furious work, before I discovered one of the templates didn't belong and the pattern won't work. So back to the beginning. Annie-Rose has sent me one of those magnifiers that you hang round your neck, in which my invisible stitches for unpicking are seen as mariner's rope on canvas. By some oversight in design the frame that

stands on one's chest allows for one central bosom, not the usual number, and so cannot be stabilised. I need six yards of wide material for the foundation. Can you possibly get me the lovely plum cotton you made my maternity tunic of? It would be perfect. I am surprised and delighted that I can still sew. If the stuff is narrow width I should need nine. What a lot they cost to make.

Another time, with cost in mind:

Bills are terrifying. Patchwork lining and repairs plus 3 yards denim for trousers cost £29!!! As you probably know, I shall have to wear tired meat at least once, and it goes with nothing I have, and never could.

In this patchwork there are twelve 16" diameter compasses, each one made with three fabrics with a different 3" circle in the centre, carefully chosen from fabric representing something to do with the sea: a lifebelt, a ship's wheel, and Paisley patterns for fish or octopus. In addition, a nautical motif has been applied to two of the centre circles. The compasses are mounted on a chestnut Madras cotton shot with navy-blue threads in the warp to make a plum-colour.

Length: 93"   *Width:* 70½"   *Templates:* Mariner's Compass set
Border: 2" band of the bright blue cotton used in Colin Tilney's Wallhanging
Lining: Seersucker with small, two-tone brown print on white which is seamed down the centre
Date: 1978 and 1979

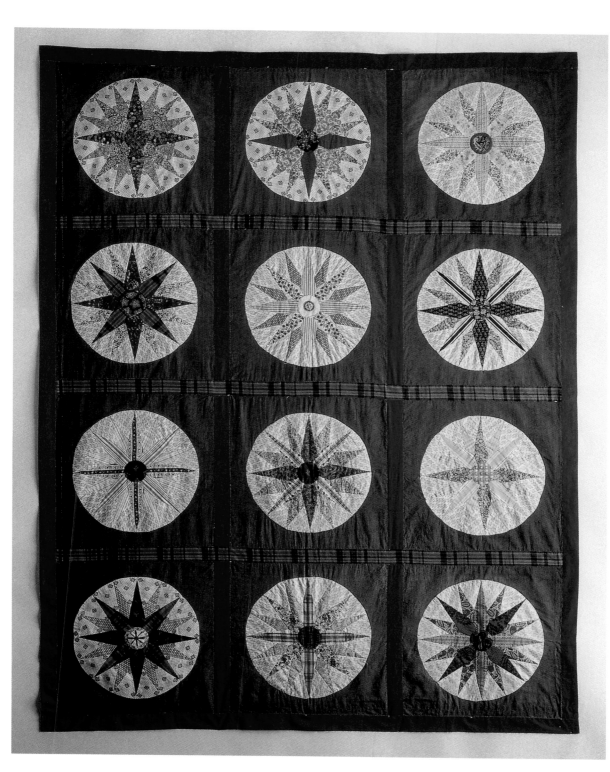

This is seamed down the middle. In another letter to Caroline Lucy wrote:

> About the patchwork – I am checkmated. I can't decide how to sew all the compasses on, whether on to an unbroken background or a lot of individual squares. Can you let me know the width of Madras cotton? And perhaps one yard to see how the colour goes in bulk.

And later:

> I never received any of that Madras cotton. Did you send it? I think four metres would do. One has to buy now because in October, when I begin sewing again, there is only wool in the shops.

And then:

> Thank you for chasing the plum colour. If I can't get it all the compasses will be adrift. I have done two more.

Each compass is in its own square, formed by three 2″ tartan bands across the width of the bedspread and two bright blue bands down the length. The appliqué of the compasses obviously caused problems, as she wrote:

> My patchwork is proving very difficult indeed. It has large circular patterns that will not lie flat. They all heave up like rising tea-cakes.

The bands are stitched on in white cotton as by this time Lucy, now aged eighty-six, was having difficulty seeing her stitches. Often one of the village children would come in and thread a collection of needles with white cotton for her. This went on for some years and there are a number of local children, now adults, who remember contributing in this way towards her patchworks. One small girl was often

This is another splendid patchwork for a grandson with bold use of
colour and pattern. Lucy did not have access to the wealth of fabrics
that nowadays is specially manufactured for patchwork enthusiasts.
Her choice was made from dress materials or furnishing fabrics and
these she collected over more than fifty years.

followed by her cat who would sit by the front door wait-
ing for her to reappear. Lucy had a horror of cats in the garden, as it is such a sanctuary for birds, so would fiercely
shoo the cat away. The child was never brave enough to say
that it was hers.

Although Lucy may have had difficulty seeing her stitches every point of the compasses is true.

In February 1979 she wrote to Caroline:

> I cannot find any possible lining for Mariner's Compass.
> We should be thankful that cotton now exists again, even
> at £2 a metre. I feared it had gone for ever.

On finishing it, Lucy wrote again,

> I so love the Mariner's Compass patchwork I hate to give
> it up to Charles. It suits this house to perfection.

Nevertheless she very generously did give it to Charles.

The Needlecord Patchwork

*T*HIS was made for Peter and me in the traditional 'Double Irish Chain'. Each of the fifty blocks is made up of twenty-five squares in various patterns using three different cotton fabrics. There are Liberty prints and Laura Ashley prints, some of which are new to this patchwork, but amongst these are many of the old faithfuls which have appeared in nearly every patchwork.

The linking Irish Chain is in pink and brown Laura Ashley needlecord. The nap lies in different directions giving the whole a warm, glowing, texture. This is the first patchwork where Lucy has mixed types of fabrics. The scale of the pieces and the setting of the blocks in the dark needlecord gives the impression of jewels in a rich setting.

In December 1979 Lucy wrote to Caroline:

Thank you for that excellent cotton. Cornwall seems to have much better taste than Cambridge.... I am so addicted to my patchwork all else is neglected, no letter written, no boggy gardening done. It is very mild, but wet and wind to rattle the house.

On 2 January 1980:

The patchwork grows and twinkles and is fascinatingly impossible and not a success. I have used up all my most treasured stuffs on it and feel therefore there can never be another. Some of these stuffs I have had since the War! They have appeared in every patchwork since.

And, a week later:

My patchwork is the dullest half-wit. It is merely an assertion that I can still nearly sew a very simple thing.

If my calculation of the order of these patchworks is correct, then this was the last, large, pieced patchwork that Lucy made.

Length: 87" *Width:* 102½" *Template:* 1½ square
Border: A 10½" border of blue Laura Ashley needlecord in four pieces folded over to form the border round the lining
Lining: Laura Ashley brown-and-white floral print with one seam, but Lucy had to insert a wedge-shaped piece as this bedcover is not quite square
Date: Probably 1979 and 1980

She writes about it:

> I have been alone for days with a gastric bug, but not too ill to go on with the patchwork, which is a dazzling creation but very slow. I doubt if I shall live long enought to finish it.

Then, in one of her rare dated letters, on 31 October 1982, she wrote:

> As I don't read any more my patchwork leaps along and to me is very exciting.

In November, a few weeks before her ninetieth birthday, while applying the stars to the squared fabric, she wrote:

> It is difficult work sewing the elaborate patchwork units on to their background. I can't do it on my lap, but must stand over a table to keep it flat. A huge double bed expanse. I am not sure I can do it.

When it was finished:

> No patchwork and what am I do to with myself?

This patchwork was given to Ron Lewcock, a friend who encouraged Lucy to continue making patchworks into her nineties.

Each of these stars measures 24" across, so it is hardly surprising that Lucy at times felt that she was unequal to the task of standing bent over a table sewing them on to the background, particularly as there are thirty of them. It was indeed a courageous undertaking for a 91-year-old and one can only feel sympathetic admiration for the occasional misalignment.

Islamic Tiles Patchwork

' RON showed me a quite wonderful Islamic pattern for tiles that would make a thrilling patchwork, and insists that I must do it,' Lucy wrote to Caroline Hemming. 'He has cut out all the templates for every conceivable variation and has bought me yards of good material, but none of it will do. It's all too English.'

Lucy then asked Peter, Caroline and Ron Lewcock himself, to draw on some of the star-shapes (with waterproof fabric paint) pictures appropriate for a patchwork inspired by Islamic tiles. She also managed to find various motifs from different fabrics for the remaining stars.

Caroline Hemming drew the fourteen pictures surrounded by a brown-check border, and Ron Lewcock the five paler ones; the other twelve formal patterns (composed of animals, fishes, birds, crabs, etc.) were drawn by Peter. All the shapes have borders to help Lucy to see when sewing

Length: 54"   **Width:** 28"   **Templates:** 1" long hexagon and a mixture invented for this patchwork
Border: Heavy blue cotton
Date: 1984

them together. This is a new variation of a Friendship Patchwork: instead of appliqué patches friends draw the pictures.

The patchwork was made as a cover for Ron Lewcock's clavichord, but Lucy never managed to finish it as her sight failed. She gave it to Ron's wife, Barbara, to finish sewing it to the border and to back it. It still retains many of the papers in the patches, some cut from the lined page of a Basildon Bond writing pad.

Lucy never compromised. At the age of 92, she could have made a patchwork similar to her simple but effective wartime designs. Instead, she embarked on piecing together the most complicated templates.

Lucy Boston
and her Life

Lucy Boston, the creator of these remarkable art patchworks, a garden of great beauty, and children's books which have become classics, was born in 1892, at Southport, in Lancashire. Her parents were vigorously strict Wesleyans, who regarded music, art, drama, dancing or even overt pleasure as wicked.

Consisting of little more than thin grey sand, the garden of the Southport house grew little but privet and laurel. Each Saturday the children were given a penny to spend as they chose. 'When in season,' Lucy recalled, 'I always bought a pansy root with one velvet flower, thrilled with the whole smell of wet paper, soil, leaf and pansy.' 'The sterility of this garden affected me from a very early age, and until I bought the Manor at Hemingford Grey forty odd years later my most recurrent dream was trying to reform that sixteenth of an acre of disappointment.'

In 1899 her father died, and when Lucy was ten years old the family moved for a year to Westmorland for her mother's health. From that moment, exposed to the miracles of undomesticated nature, her view of life was transformed. She became, then, like the children in her books, all eyes,

The Patchwork of the Crosses on a bed in the guest room at The Manor, Hemingford Grey.

ears and fingertips in a world almost too beautiful to absorb.

After being sent, with her sister Frances, to a Quaker boarding school in Sussex (as far south as possible) in the hope of correcting their north-country accents, Lucy later attended a finishing school in Paris, and from there went up to Somerville College, Oxford, to read English. After only two terms she left, volunteering instead for service in a French military hospital during the First World War.

In 1917 she married Harold Boston, whose family she had known for years as his stepmother was her cousin. Peter, their only child, is the original Tolly from the 'Green Knowe' books.

Lucy was not a born traveller, something which surprises people who visit her house, The Manor, Hemingford Grey, since it contains many examples of oriental art and furniture. She invariably suffered from travel-sickness at speeds over 25 m.p.h. Nevertheless, after the failure of her marriage in 1935, she wandered in France, Italy, Austria and Hungary, visiting the musical capitals of Europe. She had always been passionately fond of music and during this period found great solace in it. She also studied painting in Vienna under Robin Anderson and immersed herself in this for the next three or four years.

Returning to Britain in 1937, she took lodgings at 15 King's Parade, in Cambridge, where her son Peter was then an undergraduate at King's College. Here she instantly took up the challenge of painting King's College Chapel, doing several views of it from her window as well as very atmospheric paintings of the candle-lit interior during winter Evensongs. Because she was not allowed to sit in the chapel and sketch, she had to look carefully and then return to her easel in her lodgings to paint from memory.

Hearing one day that a house in one of the Hemingfords was for sale, Lucy remembered the seemingly derelict farm-house with a Georgian façade, glimpsed from the river years before in 1915. She drove out to Hemingford Grey in a taxi, along the then quiet, hawthorn-lined road, knocked on the front door of the Manor and announced to the astonished owners that she would be interested in buying it. They had only that very morning decided to sell, but had told no-one! She never did find out which house she should have gone to see.

Built in about 1130, the Manor is reputedly the oldest continuously-inhabited house in the country. For most of its history it was tenanted, the owners living in a grander house elsewhere. This probably explains why so much of the old house still stands unaltered. Lucy bought the house and spent two of the happiest years of her life restoring it, with the advice of the architect Hugh Hughes, her son Peter's help and the services of a splendid building firm.

When Lucy acquired it, the house had a malevolent reputation, and was known locally as the 'Poltergeist House'. I have recently met people who recall, in their youth, having to steel themselves even to walk past it along the river towpath after dusk. The restoration of most of its hidden original features, the removal of internal partitions and of an extra floor half-way up the music-room, seemed also to restore to the house the tranquility it still possesses today.

After its restoration, Lucy set about creating a magical garden, full of old roses and scented plants. She planted young yew trees, intending to clip them into geometric shapes. Just before the Queen's coronation she decided to make these into pairs of crowns and orbs, save one where the branches would not be shaped into either, and this she made into the 'Dove of Peace' from one of the sceptres. She also created several topiary chess-pieces.

In her sixties she wrote *Yew Hall*, a novel in which the house is the main character. Immediately after this she wrote the first of the children's books that were to make her famous. In these she recreated the Manor as the house of Green Knowe. Lucy and the house were as one. She felt she had known it from an earlier time.

She was indeed a remarkable woman. I came increasingly to appreciate all that she had achieved in her life, particularly from the age of forty-five when she bought the Manor: the restoration of the house; the pleasure given to so many people in the house by the musical evenings she held from 1941 until well into her nineties; the creation of the garden and the twenty-six topiary pieces; nineteen books; and, last but not least, the patchworks. As Kenneth East writes in *Lucy Boston Remembered:*

> Whatever she touched, whether it was literature, horticulture, topiary, needlework or simply everyday life, bore the imprint of her unerring sense of beauty and quality.